LIFE CYCLES

LINDA BUELLIS

PowerKiDS press.

NEW YORK

Published in 2017 by The Rosen Publishing Group, Inc.
29 East 21st Street, New York, NY 10010

Editor: Theresa Morlock
Book Design: Michael Flynn
Interior Layout: Mickey Harmon

Photo Credits: Cover (leaf texture) PremiumVector/Shutterstock.com; cover (image) By Laura Zenker/SinglEye Photography/Getty Images; p. 4 Kuttelvaserova Stuchelova/Shutterstock.com; p.5 (fish) aastock/Shutterstock.com; p. 5 (frog) Dinda Yulianto/Shutterstock.com; p. 5 (bird) Panu Ruangjan/Shutterstock.com; p. 5 (giraffe) francesco de marco/Shutterstock.com; p. 7 Martin Harvey/Getty Images; p. 9 Stefan Christmann/BIA/Minden Pictures/Getty Images; p. 10 https://en.wikipedia.org/wiki/File:Rosa_Smith_Eigenmann.jpg; p.11 (clown fish) Levent Konuk/Shutterstock.com; p. 11 (fish eggs) SARAWUT KUNDEJ/Shutterstock.com; p.13 (eggs) Nicky Rhodes/Shutterstock.com; p. 13 (early tadpoles) (/gallery-p1.html)/Shutterstock.com; p. 13 (tadpoles) Manfred Ruckszio/Shutterstock.com; p. 13 (frog) Matt Antonino/Shutterstock.com; p. 14 Mark Conlin/Getty Images; p. 15 https://upload.wikimedia.org/wikipedia/commons/b/b9/World%27s_Oldest_Reptile_%2815844883993%29.jpg; p. 16 ilikestudio/Shutterstock.com; p. 17 (egg) https://upload.wikimedia.org/wikipedia/commons/5/58/Monarch_egg_lgbg.JPG; p. 17 (adult) CHAINFOTO24/Shutterstock.com; p. 17 (pupa) THEJAB/Shutterstock.com; p. 17 (caterpillar) Brandon Alms/Shutterstock.com; p. 18 https://commons.wikimedia.org/wiki/File:Wilhelm_Hofmeister.jpg; p. 19 Andrew M. Allport/Shutterstock.com; p. 21 KidStock/Getty Images; p. 22 Monkey Business Images/Shutterstock.com.

Cataloging-In-Publication Data

Names: Buellis, Linda.
Title: Life cycle / Linda Buellis.
Description: New York : PowerKids Press, 2017. | Series: Spotlight on earth science | Includes index.
Identifiers: ISBN 9781499425741 (pbk.) | ISBN 9781499425772 (library bound) | ISBN 9781499425758 (6 pack)
Subjects: LCSH: Life cycles (Biology)--Juvenile literature.
Classification: LCC QH501 2017 | DDC 571.8--d23

Manufactured in China

CPSIA Compliance Information: Batch #BW17PK For further information contact Rosen Publishing, New York, New York at 1-800-237-9932.

CONTENTS

CHAPTER ONE

GROWING UP

Over the course of an organism's life, it goes through changes that mark its journey to adulthood. There are as many different ways of growing up as there are **species** in the world. A creature's life can be as short as a few days or as long as hundreds of years. Its body might look the same for most of its life, or it might change so much you wouldn't recognize it. The goal of each living thing is to survive to adulthood and to create **offspring** that can continue the species when it dies.

Animals are divided into groups based on their bodies and habits. The animal kingdom includes both **vertebrates** (such as mammals, birds, fish, reptiles, and amphibians) and **invertebrates**. By taking a look at each of these animal groups, we can study the many differences between their life cycles.

REPTILE

FISH

AMPHIBIAN

BIRD

MAMMAL

There are over 8.7 million different animal species in the world! By grouping them into categories, we are able to study the habits that are common among them.

CHAPTER TWO

LIFE AS A MAMMAL

Mammal babies **develop** inside their mother's body. Most mammals give birth to live young. A mammal's **gestation** time often depends on the size and number of babies. Some mammals, like pandas, have only one or two babies but others, like opossums, can have up to 20 babies. Once born, the babies rely on their mother for milk.

Mammal babies look like smaller adults. They grow larger in size but don't change form. Most babies stay close to their mothers, who train them to find food and shelter and to avoid predators. A mammal is an adult when it's able to find food for itself, find a **mate**, and make its own young. Seasonal changes let animals know when to go find a mate. Some mammals mate in the spring, but others mate in winter. The number of times a mammal gives birth usually depends on the length of its gestation period.

An orangutan mother raises her baby without the help of a mate. She spends eight years teaching her young one how to find food, build a nest, and survive.

CHAPTER THREE

FROM EGG TO BIRD

Unlike mammals, birds are hatched from eggs outside their mother's body. A female bird lays an egg with a hard shell. The parents warm and protect their eggs as the young develop inside them. This is called incubation. The babies break their shells from the inside using a hard part of their beak called the egg tooth.

Once they wiggle out into the open, baby birds are called nestlings. Some parents feed their young with food from their own stomachs. This is called regurgitation. The amount of time a nestling is cared for by its parents depends on its species. Over time, the nestlings grow flight feathers. When a nestling begins to practice flying, it's called a fledgling.

Once fledglings reach adulthood, they go out to find a mate. Some birds, such as bald eagles, find mates that are their partners for life. Some birds **migrate** to a different **ecosystem** each year to build their nests and lay eggs in a warmer environment.

Emperor penguin fathers hold eggs in a warm pouch under their bellies for about 65 days. During this time, penguin mothers travel out to sea to hunt. When the eggs hatch, mother penguins return to them to feed their chicks regurgitated fish.

CHAPTER FOUR

HATCHING A FISH

There are five steps in a fish's life cycle: egg, larva, fry, juvenile, and adult. Many fish eggs never hatch. Temperature changes can damage them and larger animals can eat them. Some fish parents try to protect their eggs by hiding them under plants. Since many eggs don't survive, some species of fish lay hundreds, or even thousands, of eggs!

Rosa Smith Eigenmann was one of the first female ichthyologists, which is a biologist who studies fish.

Mother and father clown fish team up to prepare their homes by cleaning them before the mother lays her eggs. While the eggs incubate, the parents clean them and fan them with their fins.

CLOWN FISH
EGGS

Before a fish is ready to find food, it feeds off a sac on its body. This is known as the larval stage. As soon as the sac has been eaten, the fish is called a fry. Now it can eat on its own. When it enters the juvenile stage, a fish must compete with others in its habitat to find a home. A fish is an adult when it can find a mate and make babies. When adult fish come together to create new eggs, it is called spawning.

CHAPTER FIVE

AMPHIBIAN METAMORPHOSIS

An amphibian spends part of its life in water and part on land. The life cycle of an amphibian is particularly interesting because most species go through **metamorphosis**.

Unlike mammals and birds, most amphibian parents don't spend time taking care of their young. Once they lay their eggs, the young are left to survive on their own. Amphibian eggs are spawned in water. While a baby is inside an egg, it's called an embryo.

Taking a look at the life cycle of a frog, we can see just how much an amphibian's body can change during its life. When it has developed enough to hatch, a young frog enters the world as a larva, or tadpole. This tadpole has gills and a tail. Over time, the tadpole grows lungs, legs, and arms. Its tail is absorbed, or taken into, its body. Depending on the species, a frog's metamorphosis can take anywhere from two months to three years.

EARLY TADPOLES

TADPOLES

EGGS

ADULT FROG

You'd never guess by looking at an adult frog how much it has changed during its life cycle.

CHAPTER SIX

REPTILE DEVELOPMENT

Some reptiles can develop fully in just one year. Others, like the loggerhead sea turtle, can take 25 years to develop into adults. Certain species have made this animal group famous for living very long lives. Right now, the oldest living tortoise is about 184 years old!

A loggerhead sea turtle makes six to eight nests per birthing season. More than a hundred eggs may be laid in each nest. With many nesting habitats destroyed by human construction, fewer of these babies survive each season.

Jonathan the giant tortoise is the world's oldest living reptile. He was hatched sometime around 1832.

No matter how long or short, a reptile's life cycle normally progresses from egg to hatchling to juvenile to adult. A few reptiles, such as boa constrictors, give birth to live young instead of laying eggs. Reptile eggs usually have soft shells and are laid on land. Most turtles, lizards, and snakes leave their young to fend for themselves as soon as they've hatched. However, the female crocodile builds a nest for its eggs, carries the hatchlings to the water after birth, and spends more than a month guiding and protecting the babies.

CHAPTER SEVEN

INVERTEBRATE LIFE CYCLES

Insects are invertebrates. They go through a life cycle called metamorphosis.

Complete metamorphosis includes four stages: egg, larva, pupa, and adult. A monarch butterfly hatches from an egg as a caterpillar, a kind of larva. Over the next two weeks, the larva grows and molts, or sheds, its **exoskeleton**. When the caterpillar is grown it enters the pupa stage. A pupa is a hard shell, or chrysalis, inside of which the butterfly is formed. It takes about a month to complete the cycle of metamorphosis, but the monarch butterfly may live only for a few weeks as an adult.

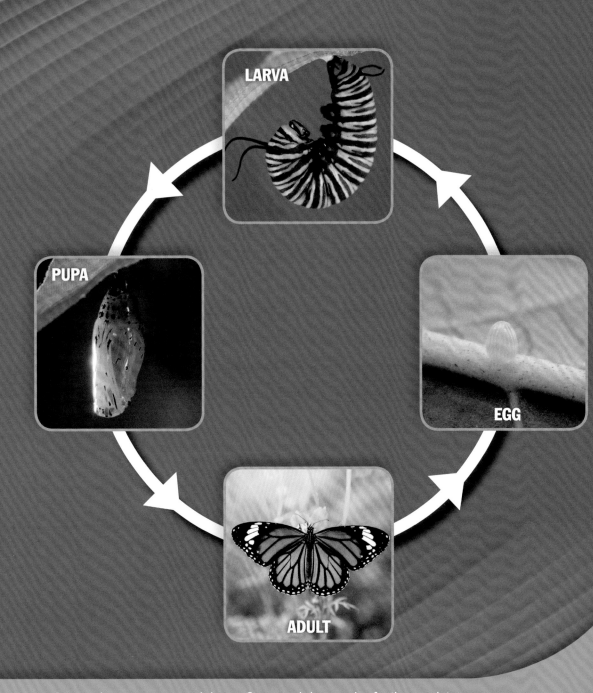

LARVA

PUPA

EGG

ADULT

During the winter, monarch butterflies travel thousands of miles south in search of warm climates. Rising global temperatures have led to habitat loss and changes in migration patterns, putting this species in danger of extinction.

CHAPTER EIGHT

SEEDLINGS SPROUTING

Just like any other living thing, a plant is created by an adult, grows, and produces offspring of its own. A flowering plant's cycle usually begins with a seed. Once the seed is buried in the ground, it begins to germinate, or sprout, as it soaks up water and warmth. During germination, the seed's hard outer layer splits open so its stem and roots can begin to grow. At this time, it's called a seedling.

Wilhelm Hofmeister was a German botanist, which is a scientist who studies plants. Much of what we know about plant life cycles was discovered through his research.

DANDELION

A seedling needs sunlight, carbon dioxide, and water to grow into an adult plant. Through the process of photosynthesis, a plant converts energy into the **nutrients** it needs to survive. A plant reaches adulthood when it begins to flower. The final cycle in a plant's life is spreading its seeds. Seeds can be spread by wind, water, or animals within the plant's community.

CHAPTER NINE

HUMAN IMPACT ON LIFE CYCLES

Think about your own life cycle so far. You are probably in a youth stage and just beginning your journey to adulthood. Just like any other living thing, you rely on resources, or things you can use, to survive. Some resources you might use today are water to drink and wash with and food to eat. Where do the resources that you use come from?

The way we use our resources affects the lives of every species in our ecosystem. There are many threats to the lives of plants and animals, and the greatest are often caused by humans. Many species are suffering because people have damaged their **habitats** or used up their resources. By thinking about how we can share our resources, or use them in a way that's healthy for the environment, we can help protect the many species of our world.

Humans produce garbage that damages the environment. You can help protect your ecosystem by being careful about the trash you create and by recycling paper, plastic, and glass.

CHAPTER TEN

BIODIVERSITY

No plant or animal completes its life cycle without affecting the life cycle of other organisms. At each stage of growth, the organism interacts with other species that can help or harm it. For an ecosystem to be healthy, it's important that many different species are present to balance each other out. Biodiversity is the number of different species in an ecosystem.

Plants supply food, shelter, and oxygen to the animal species in their ecosystems. Different animal species rely on each other for the food they need to survive. When a plant or animal dies, its body is naturally broken down into nutrients that encourage more growth. Even when one organism's life is complete, it continues to play a role in its ecosystem.

GLOSSARY

develop (dih-VEH-lup) To cause something to become more advanced.

ecosystem (EE-koh-sis-tuhm) A natural community of living and nonliving things.

exoskeleton (ek-so-SKEH-leh-tun) A hard covering on the outside of an animal or insect's body.

gestation (jeh-STAY-shun) Time when an animal is pregnant, or carrying a growing baby inside itself.

habitat (HAA-buh-tat) The natural home for plants, animals, and other living things.

invertebrate (in-VER-tuh-bruht) An animal that does not have a backbone.

mate (MAYT) One of two animals that come together to produce babies, or to come together to make babies.

metamorphosis (meh-tuh-MOR-fuh-sus) The process through which an animal changes from one body form to another.

migrate (MY-grayt) To move from one place to another as the seasons change.

nutrient (NOO-tree-uhnt) Something taken in by a plant or animal that helps it grow and stay healthy.

offspring (OFF-spring) New life or young created by adults of a species.

species (SPEE-seez) A group of plants or animals that are all the same kind.

vertebrate (VER-tuh-bruht) An animal with a backbone.

INDEX

PRIMARY SOURCE LIST

Page 10
Rosa Smith Eigenmann, American ichthyologist. Photograph. ca. 1900 to 1947. Taken by Morris in Bloomington, Indiana. Now kept at Scripps Institution of Oceanography Photographs.

Page 15
Jonathan the giant tortoise. Photograph. 2014. Taken by David Stanley in Saint Helena, a British territory.

Page 18
Wilhelm Hofmeister, German botanist. Photograph. ca. 1870. Originally published in 1905 in *The Plant World 8: 291-198* by Karl von Goebel.

WEBSITES